Childhoods
of the
Presidents

John Adams

Childhoods of the Presidents

John Adams

George W. Bush

Bill Clinton

Ulysses S. Grant

Andrew Jackson

Thomas Jefferson

John F. Kennedy

Abraham Lincoln

James Madison

James Monroe

Ronald Reagan

Franklin D. Roosevelt

Theodore Roosevelt

Harry S. Truman

George Washington

Woodrow Wilson

John Adams

Hal Marcovitz

Mason Crest Publishers
Philadelphia

Produced by OTTN Publishing, Stockton, New Jersey

Mason Crest Publishers
370 Reed Road
Broomall, PA 19008
www.masoncrest.com

First printing

1 3 5 7 9 8 6 4 2

Library of Congress Cataloging-in-Publication Data

Marcovitz, Hal.
    John Adams / Hal Marcovitz.
       p. cm.   (Childhood of the presidents)
    Summary: A biography of the second president of the United States, focusing on his childhood and young adulthood.
    Includes bibliographical references and index.
      ISBN 1-59084-268-5
    1. Adams, John, 1735-1826—Childhood and youth—Juvenile literature. 2. Adams, John, 1735-1826—Juvenile literature. 3. Presidents—United States—Biography—Juvenile literature. [1. Adams, John, 1735-1826—Childhood and youth. 2. Presidents.] I. Title. II. Series.
    E322.M35 2003
    973.4'4'092—dc21
    [B]   2002069202

Publisher's note: All quotations in this book come from original sources, and contain the spelling and grammatical inconsistencies of the original text.

Childhoods
of the
Presidents

Table of Contents

★★★★★★★★★★★★★★★★★★

Introduction 6
Arthur M. Schlesinger, jr.

"Joyfull News" 9

Braintree 17

At Harvard 25

The Prospect of Doing Good 31

All the Glory 35

Chronology 42

Glossary 43

Further Reading 44

Internet Resources 45

Index 46

★*Introduction*★

Alexis de Tocqueville began his great work *Democracy in America* with a discourse on childhood. If we are to understand the prejudices, the habits and the passions that will rule a man's life, Tocqueville said, we must watch the baby in his mother's arms; we must see the first images that the world casts upon the mirror of his mind; we must hear the first words that awaken his sleeping powers of thought. "The entire man," he wrote, "is, so to speak, to be seen in the cradle of the child."

That is why these books on the childhoods of the American presidents are so much to the point. And, as our history shows, a great variety of childhoods can lead to the White House. The record confirms the ancient adage that every American boy, no matter how unpromising his beginnings, can aspire to the presidency. Soon, one hopes, the adage will be extended to include every American girl.

All our presidents thus far have been white males who, within the limits of their gender, reflect the diversity of American life. They were born in nineteen of our states; eight of the last thirteen presidents were born west of the Mississippi. Of all our presidents, Abraham Lincoln had the least promising childhood, yet he became our greatest president. Oddly enough, presidents who are children of privilege sometimes feel an obligation to reform society in order to give children of poverty a better break. And, with Lincoln the great exception, presidents who are children of poverty sometimes feel that there is no need to reform a society that has enabled them to rise from privation to the summit.

Does schooling make a difference? Harry S. Truman, the only twentieth-century president never to attend college, is generally accounted a near-great president. Actually nine—more than one fifth—of our presidents never went to college at all, including such luminaries as George Washington, Andrew Jackson and Grover Cleveland. But, Truman aside, all the non-college men held the highest office before the twentieth century, and, given the increasing complexity of life, a college education will unquestionably be a necessity in the twenty-first century.

Every reader of this book, girls included, has a right to aspire to the presidency. As you survey the childhoods of those who made it, try to figure out the qualities that brought them to the White House. I would suggest that among those qualities are ambition, determination, discipline, education—and luck.

—ARTHUR M. SCHLESINGER, JR.

The Adams homestead in Braintree (now Quincy), Massachusetts. John Adams was born in the red house at right; he moved into the house next to it after marrying. Both structures are still standing.

"Joyfull News"

Young John Adams sat in the one-room schoolhouse in his hometown of Braintree, Massachusetts, thoroughly bored with his studies. His teacher, Joseph Cleverly, had graduated from Harvard, the best college in the colonies. But in spite of his education, Cleverly could do no better than find a job teaching in a small town. Bitter at this turn of events, he was hardly a dedicated teacher. Those who suffered most from his laziness were the bright and promising students of Braintree. John Adams was one of those students.

John enjoyed spending time outdoors. Sitting in Cleverly's classroom, he often daydreamed of hunting with the rifle given to him by his father, John Adams Sr. The boy called the gun his "fowling piece" because he used it mostly to hunt birds, which are also known as fowl. But he hunted other small animals as well, including squirrels, rabbits, and woodchucks.

He enjoyed the company of his friends Edmund and Samuel Quincy. Another friend in Braintree was John Hancock. John Adams and his friends would often play hooky from school so they could romp in the woods outside

Braintree. They hunted, played games, or pretended that the Ponkapoag Indians were fierce savages. Nothing could have been further from the truth—the Ponkapoags were friendly Native Americans who would emerge from the forests near Braintree to fish in the Neponset River or trade with the townspeople. The Indians were often met by Colonel John Quincy, the Quincy boys' father, who had been appointed Indian agent for Braintree. It was Colonel Quincy's job to see to the needs of the Indians and keep the peace with them.

Still, it was fun for John Adams and his friends to hide beneath ridges and behind trees as they spied on the Ponkapoags, imagining themselves to be brave soldiers fighting against hostile Indians. Unknown to the boys, in a few years their game would no longer be the folly of young minds. In 1754 *colonists* in America would go to war against an invading French army, which allied itself with Indian tribes anxious to reclaim their lands and push the colonists out of North America. The clash became known as the French and Indian War.

Though they might have liked, John Adams and his friends could not play hooky every day. Back in Cleverly's classroom, John struggled to pay attention. He had little trouble with most of the assignments. In fact, he'd taught himself mathematics at a much faster pace than Cleverly had been teaching.

"I applyd myself to it at home alone and went through the whole Course, overtook and passed by all the Schollars and School, without any master," John wrote later.

Actually, there was one course at school that John found difficult. It was Latin, the language of the ancient Romans. By the 1700s few people spoke Latin fluently, but it was still employed in religious services, and many of its terms were used in the education of doctors and lawyers.

By the time John was 14 years old, he could take no more of Cleverly's classroom. He told his father that he wished to leave school and join him in working the fields of the family farm. John Adams Sr. was alarmed. He knew his boy was bright and had already decided to send him to Harvard College. The Adamses were by no means wealthy—John Adams Sr. had three sons and could afford to send only one boy to college. He felt John, the eldest, was the most promising scholar of the three.

John Adams recalled, "I told him I did not love Books and wished he would lay aside thoughts of sending me to Colledge." His father replied, "What would you do Child? Be a Farmer? A Farmer? Well I will shew you what it is to be a Farmer. You shall go to Penny ferry tomorrow Morning and help me get Thatch."

John Adams Sr. was a shoemaker as well as a farmer; in the former trade he would have used leatherworking tools like the ones pictured on this table in the family's Braintree home. John Adams later wrote that his father was of "sturdy, unostentatious demeanor" and "a solid citizen."

During colonial times, farming was particularly backbreaking, but the young John Adams insisted that he would rather work in his family's fields than attend school. Eventually, his father convinced him to continue his studies.

"I shall be very glad to go Sir," John told his father.

In the 1700s, farmers knew few conveniences. Work was done mostly by hand, often requiring the men to carry heavy loads on their backs or struggle behind plows while reluctant mules dug *furrows* in their rocky fields. As the son of a farmer, John was certainly aware of the hardships that awaited him in the fields. But he insisted to his father that he wanted to leave school and take up farming.

The next morning, John Adams accompanied his father to the Penny ferry, a marshy area near the Neponset River, to gather *thatch*. They worked all day in the swampy Neponset marsh, pulling thatch and toting it back to the Adams farm. By the end of the day, John's pants were soaked with mud, his hands hurt from blisters, and his back ached from carrying the heavy loads of thatch.

That night, his father asked him, "Well John, are you satisfied with being a Farmer?"

John was not about to admit that he was wrong, especially since the thought of returning to Cleverly's classroom seemed so unbearable. "Though the Labour had been very hard and very muddy," he recalled, "I answered, 'I like it very well, Sir.'"

"Ay, but I don't like it so well: so you shall go to School," John Adams Sr. huffed, angry that the day of grueling farm work hadn't convinced his son to return to class. His father's insistence that he receive an education would prove quite fortunate for John Adams—and, as it turned out, for all of America. John Adams would become one of the key figures in the creation of the United States.

During their discussion, John finally told his father the problem—that he was bored with his studies, that he had taught himself mathematics, and that Cleverly did not seem to care whether the students paid attention in class. John decided not to tell his father that he was struggling with Latin.

"You know," John Adams Sr. said, "I have set my heart upon your Education at Colledge and why will you not comply with my desire?"

Father and son arrived at a solution. There was another teacher in town, Joseph Marsh, who provided private tutoring. Unlike Cleverly, Marsh was an enthusiastic teacher who challenged his students. In return, his students worked hard to please him. John suggested he would be willing to take private lessons from Marsh. That night, John Adams Sr. called on Marsh and arranged for the tutor to give lessons to his son.

"To this School I went, where I was kindly treated, and I began to study in Earnest," John remembered. "My Father soon observed the relaxation of my Zeal for my Fowling Piece, and my daily encreasing Attention to my Books."

John still struggled with Latin. But Marsh guided him through the lessons and, after a year of tutoring the boy, decided that John was ready to enter college. John Adams was now 15 years old. Marsh spoke with some teachers at Harvard College and arranged an interview.

To enter Harvard, John would have to appear before the college president as well as a committee of teachers and prove to them that he knew his studies. Marsh planned to attend the interview with John. But on the day of the interview, the teacher became sick and was unable to travel to Harvard with his student.

More presidents have attended Harvard than any other college or university. In addition to John Adams, they include John Quincy Adams, Theodore Roosevelt, Franklin Delano Roosevelt, Rutherford B. Hayes, John F. Kennedy, and George W. Bush.

For young John Adams, it must have been a lonely and terrifying 10-mile horseback ride from Braintree to the town of Cambridge, where Harvard is located. Forced to face the Harvard admissions committee without Marsh at his side, he was convinced he would fail and have to return home, disappointing his father.

At Harvard, he met Edward Holyoke, the president of the college, and a committee of three teachers: Henry Flynt,

Belcher Hancock, and Joseph Mayhew. Wearing powdered wigs and black robes, they sat before John prepared to question the boy on his knowledge of science, mathematics, and other subjects.

If he gained admission to Harvard, John would be enrolled in Mayhew's classes. Mayhew conducted the interview, and soon handed the boy a page of written Latin. He asked John to translate it into English.

John studied the page. Suddenly, his worst fears seemed to have been realized. John believed that he had to translate the Latin words by simply reading the paper. He recognized few of the words on the page and felt that he was on the verge of failure. He was about to tell Mayhew that he could not translate the Latin when the teacher spoke up, directing the boy to follow him to his study. He told John to sit at a desk and handed him a Latin dictionary as well as other books that would help him translate the page into English. He assured John that he could take his time, then left the boy alone to perform the assignment.

"This was joyfull news to me and I then thought my Admission safe," John wrote. "The Latin was soon made, I was declared Admitted."

And so John Adams was admitted to Harvard. He would work hard at the college in the coming years, finding himself interested mostly in studying law. His background in law would become vitally important to America as he helped lay the groundwork for the nation's independence from England and, later, when he served as the second president of the United States.

Seeking religious freedom, the Pilgrims established the first permanent English settlement in Massachusetts during the winter of 1620–21. Henry Adams, great-great-grandfather of John Adams, arrived in the colony 20 years later.

Braintree

Massachusetts was first explored by an Italian, Giovanni da Verrazano, sailing for France in 1524. Other explorers followed. In 1614 Captain John Smith led a mapmaking mission along the New England coast. In 1607 Smith had helped establish the first permanent English colony in America, at Jamestown, Virginia. But he had no interest in settling Massachusetts.

The first permanent settlement in Massachusetts was established by the passengers of the *Mayflower*, who arrived at Plymouth on December 21, 1620. They were the Pilgrims, members of a religious community who had broken away from the Church of England. They drew up the Mayflower Compact, establishing the framework for a government in their colony.

Life in the Massachusetts wilderness proved hard for the settlers, but their efforts eventually resulted in a thriving New England colony. Within a few years they were joined by other settlers from England, anxious to find religious freedom in the New World. True, they would still be under the rule of the king of England. But in Massachusetts as well as other

The front door to the five-room farmhouse in Braintree where John Adams was born and spent his first 15 years. Though he shared a cramped bedroom with his brothers Peter and Elihu, he said his childhood "went off like a fairytale."

colonies, the king seemed willing to give the colonists a large say in how they governed themselves.

John Adams's great-great-grandfather, Henry Adams, arrived in Massachusetts in 1640, settling in Braintree. The town had been named for the Braintree Company, which was formed in England in 1625 by the people who were to become the town's original settlers. Henry Adams was a farmer and maltster—he grew barley, a chief ingredient of *ale*, and ground it into a powder known as malt so that it could be brewed into the beverage.

The Adamses soon established themselves as an important

family in Braintree. Henry's son Joseph became a *selectman*, meaning he held a seat on the town council. After that, each generation of Adamses would have a member who served on the town council.

John's father, John Adams Sr., was a selectman. He also served as a *deacon* in the Braintree church. In October 1734, at the age of 43, Adams married 25-year-old Susanna Boylston. A year later, on October 30, 1735, Susanna gave birth to a son, John Adams. Two other sons, Peter and Elihu, would follow.

John Adams grew up in a five-room farmhouse at the foot of Penn's Hill in Braintree. A massive brick chimney provided heat to the home—an important consideration, given the icy New England winters the family had to endure. Even so, the house was cold in the winter. Water left in pans was known to freeze overnight.

John shared a room upstairs with Peter and Elihu. It was a tiny room with barely enough space for three beds.

When not going to school or helping his father around the farm, young John Adams enjoyed playing games with his friends. Those games are quite similar to the games children play today.

Of his childhood years, John would write: "I spent my time as idle Children do in making and sailing boats and Ships upon the Ponds and Brooks, in making and flying Kites, in driving hoops, playing marbles, playing Quoits, Wrestling, Swimming, Skaiting and above all in shooting, to which Diversion I was addicted to a degree in Ardor which I know not that I ever felt for any other Business, Study or Amusement."

Although the Adamses were upstanding, longtime Braintree residents, they weren't the most respected family in town. That honor belonged to the Quincys. Colonel John Quincy had been speaker of the Massachusetts *Assembly* and an officer in the colony's *militia*. Young John Adams looked up to Colonel Quincy, believing the great man to be a true leader and independent thinker.

"He had a high sense of accountability to the Supreme Governor of the world [God] for the trusts imposed on him, and studiously avoided an ensnaring dependency on any man," John wrote of the colonel. As president, John Adams would try to live up to Colonel Quincy's example of leadership as he headed the nation's government.

There are 20 cities in the United States named Quincy, but only the citizens of Quincy, Massachusetts, pronounce the name of their town "Quin-zee," which is how Colonel John Quincy, a town leader and selectman, pronounced his name. Residents of the other 19 Quincys pronounce the name of their towns "Quin-see."

Later, the citizens of Braintree would honor Colonel Quincy when the north part of the town split off and was named Quincy.

John Adams had many opportunities to hear Colonel Quincy speak. Each Sunday, the Adamses as well as the other Braintree families would gather in the town's Protestant church to attend religious services. Each family had its own pew, the location of which was decided by the prominence of the family in Braintree's history. The Adams pew was in the front row, across the aisle from the Quincy pew.

Interior of the First Church of Braintree, which the Adams family attended. Their pew was in the front, opposite that of the Quincy family.

The town preacher was the Reverend John Hancock Sr., father of John's boyhood friend. Hancock led services and delivered sermons that would sometimes go on for hours. But at the conclusion of services, no one was prepared to leave. The church would then serve as a town meeting hall. The deacons of the church took off their church robes, transforming themselves into selectmen. They would then transact the business of the town in public, making decisions and debating issues before every citizen of Braintree seated in the church pews. What's more, those citizens had the right to be recognized, and to add their opinions to the debates by the selectmen. Occasionally, elections for selectmen would be held at the town meetings. Most citizens of Braintree had a right to cast votes in these elections.

This form of government made a deep impression on John Adams. In England the king was absolute ruler whose right to rule was handed down from generation to generation. The kings of England held the throne under what was known as "divine right," meaning they believed God had picked them and their families to rule. The king's word was not to be defied. And the king was not in the habit of deciding what to do in front of his subjects, nor of asking for his subjects' opinions in an open meeting or resolving an issue by throwing it on the floor for a vote.

Although the town's issues would be debated in public, Braintree wasn't totally democratic. Women could not serve as selectmen. Black citizens and Indians, although permitted to attend church services and town meetings, were required to sit in the balcony.

Many issues were discussed during the Braintree town meetings. The town supported the Braintree one-room school,

Furnishings from the Adams home give an idea of the family's simple yet comfortable lifestyle.

and issues such as how to provide books and supplies as well as how to pay the teacher's salary were addressed. The town's roads had to be maintained. Also,

John Adams's younger brother Elihu died in 1775 while leading a company of the Massachusetts militia during the American Revolution.

the citizens of Braintree believed they had a responsibility to care for the poor.

The debates would often be quite loud, with angry citizens shouting their objections to the decisions by the selectmen. In 1732, the Braintree Council passed a rule forbidding citizens to stand on their seats during council meetings.

As a selectman, John Adams Sr. participated in every council meeting. His son paid close attention to the arguments of the selectmen and saw how each issue was typically handled: First, the two sides would give opposing viewpoints. Next, they would work to find a middle ground. Finally, they agreed on a compromise.

Some 30 years later, John Adams took the lessons he learned watching the selectmen of Braintree to the State House in Philadelphia, where he argued for independence from England. In March 1776, just four months before the Declaration of Independence was adopted by the Continental Congress, he wrote down his thoughts about what type of government he hoped to see emerge in the new nation.

"It should be in miniature an exact portrait of the people at large," he wrote. "It should think, feel, reason, and act like them. That it may be the interest of this assembly to do strict justice at all times, it should be an equal representation."

Harvard, America's first college, was established nearly 115 years before John Adams enrolled there in 1750.

At Harvard

When John Adams was a boy, little formal education was available to the children of the colonists. Towns such as Braintree would provide a one-room schoolhouse and hire a teacher, but it was mostly up to the students, and their parents, whether they chose to attend. Most colonists were farmers. When their boys grew older, they needed them to stay home to help in the fields. Girls were permitted to go to school, but rarely were they given opportunities to attend college.

Students who were lucky enough to go to college were sent away to study not when they reached a particular age but when their teachers considered them ready. Joseph Marsh spent a year tutoring John Adams, then declared him ready for college. And so, at the age of 15, John walked onto the *common* of Harvard, ready to begin life as a college student.

Harvard College was established in 1636—just 16 years after the Pilgrims landed at Plymouth. Now known as Harvard University, it is the nation's oldest institution of higher learning. The school, located near Boston in the town of Cambridge, was founded by the government of the Massachusetts colony. It was named for John Harvard, a clergyman who left his library and half his estate to the new institution when he died in 1638. That same year, the first classes were held at Harvard, with nine students enrolled.

By the time John Adams enrolled in 1750, the school was attracting the brightest students from throughout New England, although it did compete with Yale College in nearby Connecticut. The president of Harvard during John's years there was Edward Holyoke, a minister who left little doubt about what type of government he thought his students should work to shape once they graduated.

"All forms of government originate from the people," he said. "As these forms have originated from the people, doubtless they may be changed whensoever the body of them choose, to make such an alteration."

Other teachers at Harvard would also have an influence on John Adams. One of them was John Winthrop, a professor of mathematics and *astronomy*. Winthrop was a good friend of Benjamin Franklin, a former Bostonian who at the time was becoming influential in the government of the colony of Pennsylvania. Later, Franklin would join Adams in the Continental Congress and argue for independence.

Students at Harvard were expected to work hard. Their day began before dawn when they rose for morning prayers. Following prayers was breakfast—usually little more than biscuits and milk.

Classes followed breakfast. In John's time at Harvard, each day's classes started with a lecture, and for the rest of the day the students met with their teacher, exchanging ideas about the meaning of the lecture.

King George III of England (pictured here) and the other European monarchs ruled under the theory of divine right, which held that their authority came directly from God. At Harvard, John Adams's teachers offered a different view.

The midday and evening meals consisted of a small portion of meat, a biscuit, and a mug of cider. Dessert, when served, was usually "hasty pudding," a thin, overcooked porridge made of rye, corn, flour, and mashed fruit. Students from wealthy families frequently took their meals at *taverns* in Cambridge, but John was not rich and had to get along on what was served in the dining hall.

Evenings were set aside for study, but students with free time were known to play cards and *backgammon*—games that were forbidden on campus yet played behind closed doors. Apparently, John rarely spent his idle hours in such pursuits. He once complained that many of his friends played cards "while 100 of the best books lie on the shelves." He added, "What Learning, or Sense, are we to expect from young Gentlemen, in whom a fondness for Cards outgrows and [chokes] the Desire of Knowledge?"

John was not one to allow the 100 best books to lie on the shelves unread. He'd devoured all his family's books since first being taught to read by his father. And throughout his life, reading would remain one of his main pleasures.

When he was 14, John had received a copy of Cicero's *Orations*. Cicero was an ancient Roman statesman regarded as one of the best speechmakers in history. John read the book many times, and later in life he would become known for his ability to inspire listeners with his speaking skills.

John also liked the books of Jonathan Swift, an English writer whose works included *Gulliver's Travels*. Although children still enjoy this tale of tiny people known as Lilliputians,

An illustration from *Gulliver's Travels*, by Jonathan Swift. The book, which satirized British courts, politicians, and statesmen, was a favorite of John Adams.

Not until the eve of the American Revolution would John Adams travel outside New England. In fact, before the First Continental Congress in 1774, he rarely left his home state of Massachusetts.

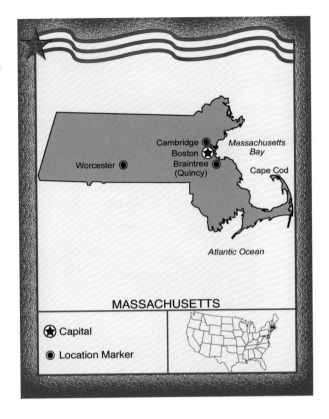

MASSACHUSETTS

⭐ Capital

◉ Location Marker

and giants called Brobdingnagians, *Gulliver's Travels* is much more than a fantasy story. The author is actually making fun of the vices, or bad habits, of people—and attacking politicians, statesmen, and other leaders of British society. Another work by Swift, "A Modest Proposal," is a bitter attack on the way England mistreated the Irish. John Adams admired Swift's courage in speaking out against injustice in British society.

Another favorite book was *The Method of Teaching and Studying the Belles Lettres*, a commentary on history written by Charles Rollin, a French priest. Essentially, Rollin urged his readers to study history—a lesson John Adams absorbed. John would soon come to see that only by knowing the mistakes of the past could people truly hope to improve the future.

This pastel drawing, done around 1766 by the American artist Benjamin Blythe, is the earliest known portrait of John Adams. By this time Adams had embarked on a law career.

The Prospect of Doing Good

ohn Adams arrived at Harvard with the intention of studying for the *ministry*. That, at least, had been his father's
wish. John Adams Sr. was, after all, a deacon of the Braintree
church.

But at Harvard, John found himself questioning his future
life as a Protestant minister. He was devoutly religious, as
were most colonists. But as a young boy he had seen his father
and the other deacons feud with the Reverend John Hancock,
questioning his judgment as well as his interpretation of the
Bible. John knew a minister's fate rested in the hands of the
members of the church, and he was afraid that if too many of
the deacons and other church members disagreed with what
he had to say from the *pulpit*, he would lose his job.

"Very strong doubts arose in my mind, whether I was
made for a Pulpit in such times, and I began to think of other
Professions," John wrote. "I perceived very clearly, as I
thought, that the Study of *Theology* and the pursuit of it as a
Profession would involve me in endless Altercations and
make my Life miserable, without any prospect of doing any
good to my fellow Men."

As a student at Harvard, John took classes in mathematics, science, rhetoric, Greek, and Latin—which, apparently, he had finally mastered. He particularly enjoyed his classes in rhetoric, which was described by the college as "the art of speaking and writing with elegance."

As he progressed through his studies at Harvard, John became more and more aware of his ability to rise in front of an audience and deliver a robust speech that would electrify his listeners. He was so good at public speaking that he soon came to the attention of the college drama club. The members of the club were not inclined to put on plays; rather, they met during the evenings to read poetry, speeches, and other dramatic works.

John attended the meetings of the drama club and found himself very much in demand as a speaker. Soon, he came to

A minister in Boston preaches to his congregation, 1700s. Although his father wanted him to pursue a religious career, John Adams said being a minister would "make my Life miserable, without any prospect of doing any good to my fellow Men."

the realization that the practice of law was not unlike the dramatic presentations he was making in front of the club members. After all, legal arguments made to a judge or jury were in their essence public speeches that often relied on heavy drama. John was intrigued by the idea of studying law.

"I was as often requested to read as any other, especially Tragedies, and it was whispered to me and circulated among others that I had some faculty for public Speaking and that I should make a better Lawyer than Divine [minister]," he revealed. "This last Idea was easily understood and embraced by me. My Inclination was soon fixed upon the Law."

But a career in the law wouldn't be an easy path. First of all, he would have to leave the friendly confines of Harvard, which in the mid-1700s had no school of law (no college in America did). Law students learned their craft by spending an apprenticeship under established lawyers. Long years of work and study awaited John Adams as he prepared for a career in the law. What's more, he would have to find a way to pay the lawyer with whom he apprenticed. John understood the hardships he would have to go through to become a lawyer. "A Lawyer must have a Fee, for taking me into his Office. I must be boarded and clothed for several Years: I had no Money; and my Father having three Sons, had done as much for me, in the Expences of Education as his Estate and Circumstances could justify and as my Reason or my honor would allow me to ask," he wrote.

Despite all this, his mind was made up. He would become a lawyer.

The BLOODY MASSACRE perpetrated in King——t Street BOSTON on March 5th 1770 by a party of the 29th REGt

Engrav'd Printed & Sold by PAUL REVERE BOSTON

Unhappy BOSTON! see thy Sons deplore,
Thy hallow'd Walks besmear'd with guiltless Gore
While faithless P——n and his savage Bands.
With murd'rous Rancour stretch their bloody Hands;
Like fierce Barbarians grinning o'er their Prey,
Approve the Carnage and enjoy the Day.

If scalding drops from Rage from Anguish Wrung,
If speechless Sorrows lab'ring for a Tongue,
Or if a weeping World can ought appease
The plaintive Ghosts of Victims such as these;
The Patriot's copious Tears for each are shed,
A glorious Tribute which embalms the Dead.

But know FATE summons to that awful Goal,
Where JUSTICE strips the Murd'rer of his Soul:
Should venal C——ts the scandal of the Land,
Snatch the relentless Villain from her Hand,
Keen Execrations on this Plate inscrib'd
Shall reach a JUDGE who never can be brib'd

The unhappy Sufferers were Messrs Saml Gray, Saml Maverick, Jams Caldwell, Crispus Attucks & Patk Carr
Killed. Six wounded; two of them (Christr Monk & John Clark) Mortally
Col by C. Remick

All the Glory

ollowing his graduation from Harvard in 1755, John Adams spent two years as a schoolteacher in Worcester, Massachusetts. Then he studied law as an apprentice to John Putnam, a Worcester lawyer. In 1758 his legal training was complete, and John opened his own law office in Braintree.

In 1764 he married Abigail Smith, who became an important adviser to her husband, often guiding his decisions. The couple's oldest son, John Quincy Adams, would follow his father into public service and, eventually, the White House. The other Adams children were Abigail, Susanna, Charles, and Thomas.

In 1770 John Adams rose to a place of prominence in the Massachusetts legal community when he successfully defended eight British soldiers charged with the deaths of five

In this famous engraving of the Boston Massacre, American patriot Paul Revere depicted a line of British troops firing into a peaceful, unarmed crowd—not exactly an accurate view of what happened. John Adams courageously defended the British soldiers involved in the 1770 incident against charges of murder.

Abigail Smith Adams, circa 1766. Intelligent and insightful, she was her husband's most trusted adviser throughout his life. This pastel portrait, like the one on page 30, was done by Benjamin Blythe.

American colonists during a riot in the streets of Boston. The incident is known as the Boston Massacre.

Simply taking the case showed a great deal of courage, as the presence of British troops in Boston was extremely unpopular. Yet John believed that everyone accused of a crime was entitled to be defended by a lawyer and have a fair trial. At the trial, John argued that the soldiers had fired on the rioters in self-defense. The jury agreed. Two of the soldiers were found guilty of a minor charge, while the other six were found not guilty.

Although the court's decision seemed like an important verdict for British rule, John was certainly no advocate for remaining under the king's hand. He believed strongly in independence. In 1775 he was elected to the Continental

Congress as a delegate from Massachusetts. While serving in the Congress, John was responsible for winning the appointment of George Washington to head the Continental Army.

In 1776 he was named to the so-called Committee of Five by the other delegates to the Continental Congress. The committee was given responsibility for framing the Declaration of Independence. The job of writing that document fell to Thomas Jefferson, a delegate from Virginia. Jefferson and Adams became great friends but years later would have a falling-out over political differences.

In Philadelphia, John Adams was the most vocal supporter of the Declaration of Independence during the Continental Congress debate in late June and early July of 1776. Using his gift for stirring speech, John was able to convince many hesitant delegates to vote for independence. The Declaration of Independence was adopted unanimously, or without a single vote against it.

Still, there was a measure of bitterness in the experience for John. In addition to helping sway the vote to break away from Great Britain, John had contributed significantly to the content of the Declaration of Independence. Yet he felt his important contributions were not recognized. He always believed that Jefferson took too much credit for the draft of the Declaration of

Abigail Adams wanted her husband to include a provision for women's rights in the Declaration of Independence.
"Remember the ladies, and be more generous and favorable to them," she told John. In the end, though, women's rights were not addressed in the Declaration.

Independence. "Jefferson ran away with the stage effect . . . and all the glory of it," he said.

During the American Revolution, John Adams served as a *diplomat* in Europe, convincing foreign allies to support the colonies. He also helped negotiate the peace treaty with England that ended the war in 1783. He remained in England as a diplomat until 1788, then returned home to run for president. He finished second to George Washington. Under the terms of the U.S. Constitution in effect at the time, he was awarded the vice presidency.

Over the years, many American vice presidents have complained about their jobs, saying that there is really very little for them to do. That was certainly true in John Adams's day. He wrote, "My country has in its wisdom contrived for me the most insignificant office that the invention of man contrived or his imagination conceived."

When Washington retired, John Adams won election to the presidency. He took office in 1797, moving into the President's House in what was then the nation's capital, Philadelphia. As president, he narrowly avoided war with France when he outmaneuvered the French in what became known as the XYZ Affair. French pirates had been encouraged by their government to attack American merchant ships trading with

John Adams suggested that July 2 be celebrated as Independence Day. That's the day delegates to the Continental Congress approved a resolution calling for independence from England. Instead, Congress declared Independence Day on July 4, the day the Declaration of Independence was adopted.

The Committee of Five, including John Adams, Thomas Jefferson, and Benjamin Franklin, presents the Declaration of Independence to the Continental Congress. Adams played a major role in shaping the famous document, and in winning for it unanimous approval.

England. President Adams sent diplomats to meet with the French foreign minister, Charles Talleyrand, but Talleyrand insisted the diplomats meet first with three of his aides. The aides demanded a bribe of $250,000 from the Americans. This demand outraged President Adams, who referred to the three Frenchmen as "X," "Y," and "Z." Members of Congress urged the president to declare war with France, but John knew the American navy was not prepared to fight sea battles with the powerful French forces. Instead, he negotiated a treaty with the British that guaranteed protection for American merchant ships and convinced Congress to halt trade with France.

By 1800, France was ready to settle its differences with America. John sent a peace mission to Paris, which angered

This portrait of John Adams was copied from a canvas John Singleton Copley painted after the Revolutionary War, when Adams served his country as a diplomat in England.

his political enemies, including Thomas Jefferson. This set the stage for a bitter presidential campaign.

Later in 1800, John and Abigail Adams moved into the new executive mansion in Washington, D.C., which was now the nation's capital. The mansion was known as the President's House then. Today we call it the White House. Although it had been under construction for eight years, the President's House was a mess when the Adamses moved in. Few of the mansion's 30 rooms were complete, the main staircase had not yet been built, and no firewood had been stockpiled for the coming winter.

"Not one room or chamber is finished of the whole," Abigail Adams wrote to her sister. "It is habitable by fires in every part, thirteen of which we are obliged to keep daily, or sleep in wet and damp places."

President Adams spent his first day in the White House conducting the business of the country. He met with visitors in his office before eating a quiet supper. Then, carrying a single candle in the dark mansion, he walked up the back stairs to the bedroom. The next day, he wrote the words that would eventually be carved into a White House mantel: "I pray Heaven to bestow the best of blessings on this house, and on all that shall hereafter inhabit it. May none but honest and wise men ever rule under this roof!"

In the election of 1800, John Adams lost a close vote to Thomas Jefferson. After leaving Washington, Adams returned to Massachusetts, where he retired to his farm.

When he died in 1826, at the age of 90, his last words were: "Thomas Jefferson survives." But John Adams was wrong. Jefferson—his fellow patriot, longtime friend, and bitter rival—had died a few hours before.

John Adams and Thomas Jefferson both died on July 4, 1826—the 50th anniversary of the adoption of the Declaration of Independence.

CHRONOLOGY

1735 John Adams is born in Braintree, Massachusetts, on October 30.

1749 Studies with private tutor Joseph Marsh.

1750 Enrolls in Harvard College.

1755 Graduates from Harvard and begins working as a schoolteacher.

1758 Opens law practice in Braintree.

1764 Marries Abigail Smith.

1770 Defends eight British soldiers charged in the Boston Massacre.

1774 Serves as a Massachusetts delegate to the First Continental Congress

1775 Joins the Second Continental Congress.

1776 Signs the Declaration of Independence.

1783 Negotiates peace treaty with England.

1788 Elected vice president.

1796 Elected president.

1800 Moves into the White House; defeated in reelection bid by Thomas Jefferson.

1826 Dies in Quincy, Massachusetts, on July 4.

ale—an alcoholic drink similar to beer.

assembly—a lawmaking body of a state, composed of representatives elected by the people.

astronomy—the study of the planets, stars, and other objects in space.

backgammon—a board game employing dice and game pieces similar to checkers.

colonists—a group of people who settle in a new land and form a community.

common—an outdoor public area, often on the grounds of a college.

deacon—an official of a church who is below the priest or minister.

diplomat—a representative of a nation sent to a foreign country to speak for his or her government's interests.

furrow—a narrow groove made in the ground where crops are planted.

militia—a nonprofessional fighting force composed of private citizens, usually organized by a state or local government.

ministry—the religious profession.

pulpit—a platform in church where religious leaders stand and read or preach.

selectman—a person elected to a board of officials governing a New England town.

tavern—in colonial days, a place where travelers could find food, drinks, and lodging.

thatch—straw used as roofing material.

theology—the study of God or religion.

FURTHER READING

Butterfield, L. H., ed. *The Adams Papers: Diary and Autobiography of John Adams*. Cambridge, Mass.: Belknap Press, 1962.

Lukes, Bonnie L. *John Adams: Public Servant*. Greensboro, N.C.: Morgan Reynolds, 2001.

McCullough, David. *John Adams*. New York: Simon and Schuster, 2001.

Peabody, James Bishop, ed. *John Adams: A Biography in His Own Words*. New York: Harper and Row Publishers, 1973.

Smith, Page. *John Adams*. Garden City, N.Y.: Doubleday and Company, 1962.

- http://www.whitehouse.gov/history/presidents/ja2.html
  The White House Biography of John Adams

- http://www.whitehouse.gov/history/firstladies/aa2.html
  The White House Biography of Abigail Adams

- http://www.history1700s.com/page1105.html
  Information on the XYZ Affair

- http://www.nara.gov/exhall/originals/declarat.htm
  Declaration of Independence (National Archives and Records Administration)

- http://www.harvard.edu
  Harvard University

- http://ci.quincy.ma.us/htm/quincy.htm
- http://www.quincymass.com/
  Quincy, Massachusetts

INDEX

Adams, Abigail (daughter), 35
Adams, Abigail Smith (wife), 35, 40
Adams, Charles (son), 35
Adams, Elihu (brother), 19
Adams, Henry (great-great-
    grandfather), 18
Adams, John
    and American Revolution, 15, 23,
        26, 38
    birth of, 19
    childhood games played by, 9–10,
        19
    death of, 41
    defends British soldiers after the
        Boston Massacre, 35–36
    early exposure of, to politics,
        21–23, 26
    education of, 9, 10, 11, 13–15,
        25–29, 31–33, 35
    as farmer, 11–13, 41
    as member of the Continental
        Congress, 23, 26, 36–38
    as president, 15, 20, 38–41
    studies law, 33, 35
Adams, John Quincy (son), 35
Adams, John Sr. (father), 9, 11, 12, 13,
    14, 19, 23, 31
Adams, Joseph (great-grandfather), 19
Adams, Peter (brother), 19
Adams, Susanna (daughter), 35
Adams, Susanna Boylston (mother),
    19
Adams, Thomas (son), 35
American Revolution, 38

Boston, 25, 36
Boston Massacre, 36
Braintree, Massachusetts, 9, 10, 14,
    18, 19, 20, 21, 22, 23, 25

Cambridge, Massachusetts, 14, 15, 27

Church of England, 17
Cleverly, Joseph, 9, 10, 11, 13
Continental Congress, 23, 26

Declaration of Independence, 23,
    37–38

England, 17, 18, 22, 23, 38, 39

Flynt, Henry, 14
France, 10, 38, 39, 40
Franklin, Benjamin, 26
French and Indian War, 10

Gulliver's Travels (Swift), 28–29

Hancock, Belcher, 15
Hancock, John Sr., 21, 31
Harvard, John, 25
Harvard College, 9, 11, 14, 15, 25–26,
    27, 31, 32, 33, 35
Holyoke, Edward, 14, 27

Jamestown, Virginia, 17
Jefferson, Thomas, 37, 38, 40, 41

Marsh, Joseph, 13, 14, 25
Massachusetts, 9, 17, 25, 35, 37, 41
Mayflower, 17
Mayflower Compact, 17
Mayhew, Joseph, 15
Method of Teaching and Studying the
    Belles Lettres (Rollin), 29
"Modest Proposal, A" (Swift), 29

Neponset River, 10, 12

Orations (Cicero), 28

Penny ferry, 11, 12
Philadelphia, 23, 37, 38

INDEX

Pilgrims, 17, 25
Plymouth, 17, 25
Ponkapoag Indians, 10
Putnam, John, 35

Quincy, Massachusetts, 20

Smith, John, 17
Swift, Jonathan, 28–29

Talleyrand, Charles, 39

Verrazano, Giovanni da, 17

Washington, George, 37, 38
Washington, D.C., 41
White House, 40–41
Winthrop, John, 26
Worcester, Massachusetts, 35

XYZ Affair, 38

Yale College, 26

PICTURE CREDITS

Contributors

ARTHUR M. SCHLESINGER JR. holds the Albert Schweitzer Chair in the Humanities at the Graduate Center of the City University of New York. He is the author of more than a dozen books, including *The Age of Jackson*; *The Vital Center*; *The Age of Roosevelt* (3 vols.); *A Thousand Days: John F. Kennedy in the White House*; *Robert Kennedy and His Times*; *The Cycles of American History*; and *The Imperial Presidency*. Professor Schlesinger served as

Special Assistant to President Kennedy (1961–63). His numerous awards include the Pulitzer Prize for History; the Pulitzer Prize for Biography; two National Book Awards; the Bancroft Prize; and the American Academy of Arts and Letters Gold Medal for History.

HAL MARCOVITZ is a journalist for *The Morning Call*, a newspaper based in Allentown, Pennsylvania. His other books in the CHILDHOODS OF THE PRESIDENTS series include biographies of Theodore Roosevelt, John F. Kennedy, and Bill Clinton. He lives in Chalfont, Pennsylvania, with his wife, Gail, and daughters Ashley and Michelle.